HERE HIGH NOTE, HIGH NOTE

HERE HIGH NOTE, HIGH NOTE

CATHERINE BLAUVELT

Thanks for chris!
the celebration!
It was so great to
read with you!
High notes to
the moon!
Catherine

PRELUDE

The Prelude Press LLC
PO Box 110593
Brooklyn, NY 11211

Stu Watson and Robert C.L. Crawford, Publishers

Designed by Mike Newton

preludebooks.com
preludemag.com

Library of Congress Cataloging-in-Publication Data has been applied for.

ISBN 978-0-9907030-5-1

For Mom

CONTENTS

HERE HIGH NOTE, HIGH NOTE

All Awning And Bugles, Still I Hope You Nearness

Light Light Vert From Mud. The charming flash
of grass flowers here on earth, the whiteless
flames without risk. My mystery flower
you walk, raise your head. As it happens,
Mad Grass Wants Us By Name. I wanted some
not much. A light strobe wedging a way lint
green, a place to put our heads. Only not,
time refolds the bugles' leak. Constant is
the view of Delirious. A hunting
sound. Lightning on a blond ocean went
the hounds in thousands for pure grass. Two blue
jays for a moment disturb their aim, knocking
the shadow out of me, only once to go out.

Whom Love Pries Paisley Apart

I leapt with fuchsia and called
   for better times. I couldn't see

   under crab grass,
   under
redhead plash. Once the birdbox
fell from sill
   to bluedrift. A sun far
      from shirtless.

            She shook her head
               and let an eye loose.
   Once the toucan was hungry

and without hair, to frill
   its neck out to sea.
   Once the redhead
      waterbugged
        for me.

I fell to a shape; "Under legs
   I'll come too. Short distance,
   accept my plant.
Nearly yes,
   only you."

Lo Lo Lo La Waiting Droops, Page Not Found

The sound of their held unknotted a day.
The hue overwhelms their cheeks. It's that hot;
"all normal eyes suddenly see green." It's that
hot beyond the image. No one to do
not in love. At their centers a small black
dot made of paint and no one else. Thus blur,
thus waiting. (I use your sleeve and awe.) The
night's imagination—an artist whose
medium is light pixel: gold seed distraction.
The image always has the last word. What
kind of green results? It can't be arranged—
white flecks alike a complement of red.

The path's too busy of black before—
thus, waiting, waiting, to end the touch.

Loll Look Without Our Legs, How Artful

the royal blue chicken, the white cat
for Joan. White space don't crowd the green
tries to escape the bird the symbol
of grass. Repeatable lace where we went
without saying it left a want. A thought
for another: many black stumps, three rose
stumps yelling out their necks existing
above them. Even without the lake the
orange slides. I want a lion to come out
of it. I do not believe Joan when she
tells me Sunflowers. She is above the
lake she comes from. White over the yellow
pink robe before the freed green still in
the air. Notice the crushed ivory sheep.

Umbel A Blizzard

              in each rhubarb stuck stalk,
        for I no longer herald their swing to
        flamingo legs.
                Shot from the half dark
diamonds that waive their away; I've pressured
blitzen in those who have quit their fission
knowing still lets the solar unshatter
the shady half.
        Mynah Nomore,
your beat-
empty organs mite madness our porching
possibilities; once standing and smooching,
you now tempt the worms looting.

                 Mine above
        the grounded; my beat-plenty organs amp
        cupids to you.
                I'm perennially in
croon, I'm left and unpruned, I'm here hushing
on a whiteout to lose direction from you.

O Yellow Flowers

After Austin Dobson's "To Daffodils"

O yellow flowers, tend my empire.
O yellow flowers, strung from one lung
to one lung; assail. Now, know it fondly,
how the mind knows to gallop

to a lady and the elate day.
O yellow flowers, tend my empire.
O yellow flowers, strung from one lung
to one lung; assail. Shall over

the morning amongst the dust of glee
and the dust to be. Awe, I have you
now. And I will, I will hunt. And I will,
I will travel with you towards her.
O yellow flowers, tend my empire.

Butterscotch Snot In Pine Tree Weeds,

many sunbeams.   High love bunked,
find us
      birdbrained.

        Find us
           ear-merry, flinch many. Leap out
green birds, green meat from the wind;
      a lot to be grass at our side. We should.
We should. Our heads
this way and calm to be no sea.

The love bit, a l*ck fl*ck.

Asterisk's the hurdle.
Two tusks in the myrtle
        pixelate.
          Flounce.
          Together, then let go.
This way,
there are pounds of seaweed in bloom.

Sod Somewhere It's Part For Me And Plant

For You Stay here to be shaped Blotch Left in
sight as possibility On the breeze little
and heaven behind Isn't but lots
Occur for a rise Plink and crimp come to me
The first time Bust loose in a description
of Motors The sky you're kidding Sea Gleam
you're not hiding Heights Spread to happen From sod
spaced like feathers In moment There I see
them As black Neon Trees No Park competes
for sod to happen A deck soon a room
with punctuation Would do so much for what
we do without blare Pound cake Heavy
and bright hang Break out in night's plot

Stand Still Gentle Blue In The Middle Blue

For Ellsworth Kelly

I'm stealing your title *Black Ripe*. Warm air.
Hunks. Fey. The weight of each shadow. Come
and watch till you find the end of the line.
I'll lie on the staircase. White overing.
Ought to be one word. Variations
of the eye. Scrolling. The blue streak fluke made
it out. The tongue gets all over; the yell-
ow is more like a flower. A pigment
reacting to light. I like the idea
of paradise. We have enough dirt. Me
away. Form me. The risk of abstraction.
The present tense. The notice it makes bloomed
out. Night shifts. It's a new language. I'm com-
pletely abstract. Bush. Yank. Organizes

the evening's end. Something you can reach up
out. *Blue (for Leo)*. I'll forgive your *Red
White*. I do. I end. A vocal cord cut loose.

Not The Nearer Unsaid Veering Drop

Tinge Like This. Elope one from before; yell-
ow curve try the window. The bathers need
to be interrupted; unrecognizable
forms on their own; unsuitable sunlight;
planar drawn into a vow. I do not
know I do. White underpainting. Blue squares
bulk over orange. The woman who brought me
here looks happy but not often. Upward;
the fig on the branch isn't a surprise
but something I can carry out. Her eye
a grafted tree. An illustration. The
Stendhal effect erased. Later I tried
to see her out of this world. In another
language TOTE. There's nothing here to stop her.

Had Everything Without Shadows Unset

my thought; I thought that cloud was the sun and
wished it for a second when. When let
my bright be body bright future. Somehow
roses change the subtitles. We are to
gether. Her arms around me. That dear shape
an empty bucket marked orange roses.
A branch in my way joy. Gold beyond white
for no reason. My own park nowhere
near this. Celebrated cauliflower
puffs; looking up in a parking lot. Too
many vases waiting unimportant
paths to Eden. Even color has
speech. Can you hear the space in the day?

What's Not Our Now Speaking People Having

Only I Was Unreal The day again
describing sooner to mud Day pet Every
light on at home—looks an unset sun You
   …on you…me…like I…you…on Copies in…
my hand before night-love Taking forever
while she picks up Time Breath wearing wake Rhymes
with silver Blue field Your mud me like Now
I have mud lingering over lights Each vowel
the sky—a sun under sound This and he
or she—me too! the tour guide Hear repurposed
mots? Easy pantones Eyes Dye cut from the
take We make the tell Use isn't
If hands in hands we do it doesn't matter
Cloud matter What's not our now Scene Undo

Lovesick Come Without A Horizon Plunge.

In full sunlight, nothing at eye-level
blocking me out. Two hues prove my eyes; tree
rot and violet-wheeze. Now, I'm standing in
your shadow's mass. Clouds intersect colors.
Deeper keys of blue convince artificial
light. My pattern canceled. The wind's off to
spring. Hours without longing you cloud-fill.
A mood ring. Gravity's my thought. Grass un-
seen, so in the freeze. I'll dip my bare legs.
A goose darker than light's weight witnessing
shade. You'll see me again. What do I impossible
flock out? Sweet you this juniper chord.
The grass enjoys but doesn't own. The sky
posing in blue expanding, follows me.

She Is With You Finding Was. Right Angles:

sound without a moon. The sky redecorated
keeping you in mind. Drawings of heaven.
Silence airbrushed. So much my life. I went
looking for a hammer. She is with you
finding was. The other side of a waterfall.
A good last line. Blotched blue colored paper.
Two plants on a window sill talking, just
friends, passing time. A bronze bust entitled
"After". A question mark garden. If
you, no one is. Your love for need by one
self. The back of the brain goes past the
elevator and makes a right—some place
to be. A repeated use of precisely
the same color. The moon is on her way.

The Honey Lump Watched From Here Goes On

Without Without. Late Only O And Married,
Sell Me Light. Field waiting lid, will does
a way. Coil, do I, do I? I'll put my light

in a vase. Outside, growless rain flapping
as it hits the pavement. Thousands of white
birds going nowhere—unsnow. Indigo
thumps. I'll say one breath: coo. Doing, I Fling
my mouth at the moon. Almighty arm and
leg splashing night where she loves. Parsley
lulu rug, pulse. No, Shadow, I don't need you.
Forgotten air, I fling my mouth at the moon.
Gold-Clear While, yes, I'll hold. Move the line
to my fingers. Before the world, hear
the distance when she appears Whole.

Lit Up White White Dead Hot Peacock Haste-

nings hysteria. Can't tell, less lovely
  either deem till we fury or as once
    wasted, glimpse cruels.

                      Each other day-clinging
wilt each as this day could mare sped herward.

Wilt hearty, broth mouth to broth mouth: juni-
    per tar shape shape your fiery give; angle
      from sea, scorching silent sorrowful ivy.

    Meet me thunder beat insist, pine through
      the blue flash; be so tramp, so swan at night. Stay with me

                              total seashore, blue waiting
                      chimes again against the dear. Clary fur-

        therer, on my way up blue veins the glove
              sluggishly to the alluvial buck-
        lings, high uncrammed unpearlings aboving me.

Shake The Sing Lightly None Talk. Didn't

a come thing Loud Out, Owl Girl. Owl. Owl. Spit-
off. Mornings Crinkle Bright Paper Bits Flame
the thump she wound to a cluck. Quick bluish
broth is the lick lowered over Night shirt,
the sky sent to twigs. Whack. Melon Ball
Spangle Flashes. The bucket set out to
collect. Drops scald instead of hold. Her Soak
upsets her vase. Her ears sit, public gardens
give out, lifting once by inches. Is she
waving? I am nodding, my loves keep up.
Loosen them from twigs. I have no windmills.
I can only think our see-make swash. Avoiding
the columns, she decides the sky marble
harvest; flies in gauze, dots hot to turn stalks.

The Day Itself, It Selves With Me So

Grass patch paradise,
no bigness. The good
sounds,
       enamors. Eyedrift out-

lets thrush down my bugles, my heart,
                 my throat-
whelms kneeling in grass. Mine to keep, convulse.

Leg Me. Light Thing I Look At Bowl, Skin Width

my hand as knots hold flowers where she moves.
Draw me limb, shooting to often The En-
trance. I knelt to become want's body. Cold
at the greenhouse without curtains. Down went
her hair in our place. We put hands at her
side. She doesn't turn. I ply the pins in her hair.
           Soon opened on a melon ball
arranged the blur, threw flew out of our heads,
the size of our head wail. Somewhere took her,
stillness. I was reaching before our heads
lit up. I need a couch. Bone, floral slip
to top.
       Keep come of us. We lie. Lift. You
watch our heads left out by a waterfall.

Ceiling Hooks Saw Her Crab Legs Soak. We Got

Here By Bending
    The Pattern.   We find ourselves making
      a ring

        grow to the ground
in the same way fire, the hottest
          bulk.

                Please your mouth
        toward stone. Hot make do. Patio.

          I'm over the floral rug.
            Have it.

I wait. The view has
a top weep swelter.

Over It Ivy Trimmings Placed So

if you look, you look
 to them hanging a window
    pane. Geese influence the sky. Who takes one,
     and too there is all. Let spill plant.
 If they do, blocks in the view resolve,
 making us visible points
  arranged to spread in. That is court.
   Count the lowest
  and few of us set. Not so
 much fanned out to let a place
be it.
Upward
goes.

Not you. Keep coming out.

Ode To Gravity

I have known you for a little while now
Sky, and with you my throat orchards. Few flowers
Remind people of bugles. I forgot. I
Left her poinsettia leaves. I put my eye-
Lids to heaven, Nina-boltz, Nina-boltz.
I put my eyelids to heaven, yet navy
Moons my thoughts. Clear night with spray paint, no one's
Like you, like you animal. Land cherries
And tigers, so well, so well. Nina you
Need a little sword for a little feast.

While eve lightlessly lifts everything up, up
And up, Gravity I'm glad I live with you
And only. No calamity, nor drummed
Up love in my nocturnal internal.

Till Morning My Head And Why

What lips little wild sing, vanish boughs
more one by one.
            Sky, you had to be leopard,
nary a dark gut full, graceflint.
            Millions
  slouching doily away, plainly about
 for others. However, in begins mute
bolster to my oblivion bling booth,
goin': pavo pavo pavo a can
of heart of palms.
            What taupe hopes much near nears
the hand? And with head! Farmed all

            farmed in you you eveing,
          chrissy sporadic clear grass
and clear. Which folly listening like shut fell
 us high-
  hearted icily when in com-
    pletes approaching?
           Neigh, I was wrong for bed
close to the day. Here High Note, High Note.

A Clara In My Throat Smash Wholes Us Lovely

Hawthorn besides you, mere mouths my leaning.
The young lungish wanna splurge. I, too,
long. Birdshit. Let not well, until shouts you
delightful cockatoo. I wanna hold
on upon neck. Hot iota. On least
flown, off a ramus sudden, at a rabbit. O
some living ellipses! See through, hollow
through thrust, and she due. O come again, the
porch is getting night. Dart. And because swept hot
the belongs to us. Bent bodies wanna
part, set sounds among the look-hunting crowd
of light. Hawthorn besides you: thumps, punch-
outs, the if stops who hurry up homely.
The neck eludes knee. Puffs puff. Hulas hoop.

Voice: Red Turnip, Unnoticed Float, Crown On

a wet bob, an occasion for weeding
the tops of waves, Styrofoam plates, say
hello. She gathers I love how it looks
her voice moved like wet hair. Sky built of wind
now is gone, and then go my limbs: Youth Pops.

Sudden the bud; in example I'm dead
counting pebbles; the rabbit stays by me
and eats. Have this enormous invisible.
Take and then breathe out wants out: two rabbits
bud long summers. Did I ask her? Without
saying it, have. A leg settles in
a delicate god. A maple tree
finds its way in a flower pot, finds
its parentheses drink until wood wilts.

Hurryin' Green And Dress

in the sweet un
eyestrobe
shut taupe. A shore
           totters,
choristers. A beach fill
ed with sheep. And water a hun
k, be

gin lagoons.

Beached Bird Decoy

In beck, hands
land; sober

germed lurches
squirm.
       Sea tangle,
dingle unraveled.

Fleet flesh carry
the undistressed

sill way on fell.

Land Me On Touch You Nude To Have Slept Sprang

Drank Bud. Bud punctures the breath. Blitz. The cloud
is budding resemblance. Grasses to be un
announced are pulled out. Love not grasses with
their withers; an entrance drank, decided the
litter. My brain is one part bale and one
part wick. The heel of one thing inspired by sip.
Move and more time. Whose tongue? One sash to be
schlepped. I soon its way; build the pulse outside
the body, clip at hind legs, nip at the naughty.
Walk from while the sunblaze made opposite.
Attention propels the lily flailing in
ponder. Do believe with the knowing. Is this
my stoop? Could do; covered with insects, strata
beings take them down. Scrunch. Bite down.

Nautilus And Spade,

we glean as almost any other mostly.
Sudden to pinwheel at somite.
Panicled
      mingo,
            hysteria mingles us so.
We sway unless lassoed,
             so long
longing.
Fuchsia's insomniacs
seek soma us hype-heartedly;

quiet still synchronized splendors in
our lung filled eyes.
            Retinacular swinging
little doors;
hibiscus lures. We stray in doors.

Sung Many After, Each Grey Gull Mistletoes

You whom. We by love bite. Eggplant. Legish,
bugish, mammals too pavilions. Furl. So
say it gone from wilderness. For likeness,
we are massy, one leap and close. Hours
of ours, a heat burring our head-down
a clearing. Crossed legs in row create
a slanted meadow. We look up the hills
here, so hounds look to the shooting trills. Cut
Young Chords come to our heartworms. Hack-hock. Slug-
smooch. How many grey gulls crouching in
a clearing? Eyeballing, not nary. Enough
noel those nearest lone. Then Sudden
flounces little hills. And we lip lip under their frill.

On The Lip Trying To Keep The Rest Full

Gossamer Motion makes way as it does
coming on in shape. Mechanical Seconds.
Get in. Get off. I'm getting to its cir
culation. Twigs Loosen. Thing think thing.
For the human bunch We're going to like
this if that doesn't sound. Twigs. Instruments
for picking; not ruining the eyes. Forms in
smashing shape. Again and again harping;
not ruining the eyes. Then I got a lighter.
Unexpectedly. To undo like this
but not now. Now is beautiful. The lit
tle pile without a fire but soon. Zilch.
Sit alone, the moon will come behind the Twigs.

Magenta In Bits, A Flower From The Ceiling Set

My eyes broad day light to fountain geese,
  making me this place. From the ceiling,
   my eyes   are not up there.
   Broad day   light is covered with us
to fountain. Geese form into what else Exhausted,
  Wanting to walk its surface,
    glimmer
     its common Outward.
             Said beneath
each beam,
  Two Dales cuss flower markets: swerves out of blue thighs.
             Their scene came here

without rest, geese tails in the ground
  flower. There, shape has a group
   soft and heavy. Pull.
             She wraps
             her arm around the plant

             to complement her mouth.

Bluff Again Bring Along, The Landscape Is

out in this, for long away ours will be
the pink above the trees below the clouds:
my throat, my untwist in the Eternal

Intricate. I back away along
the sunset. Talk awake a fire clearing
sleep heads up high. Clipped, the dandelions
are living, laughing with the sound of glue.
Polka dots and ham. The sheep left the

poet. Did the tree make a noise? I looked
up the mouth missing the head; the grass
surrounds the tree. Us into night: blue poofs
above green white a woman drawn in
black with a man. Again, voices though
no lip; early of me that love us.

Blue Smolder Parched But Otherwise Often

unlike the brushstroke; each again you. Lone
at midnight. Either direction: a sun-
set in the act starts behind the black ramp.
A series of shadows, but whom are they
attached to? I'll propose a want. The mix-
ture's boundaries: white upward, a season or
citation unthinking to be staying, to be
nobody. Your reflection gold clash defines
movement further. Up is white no air in the air;
a mixture just as clearly, more white removed
from your hands nor existing. If I ask the
negative space, a lover goes, "Please," stops
the window from breaking—admits another
day; tomorrow begins everything.

Blue-Sit Kikis Off
A Hill Of Iceberg Lettuce.

So
varicose be
neath clement
our clouds
fried
pastures of affect
ion
some in
fence

some in

shade   Now we animals
throughout

the day
affection.

Horn stuck and on
land.

Keep me

After coming.

Don't. Don't. Don't. Some Blush By

                        the remember
rabbit hole forms good times. Don't. Don't. Don't.

Everyish and done. Clamor looking exactly slug;
 cordless rose our keeps.

            Somewhere, today
   fronts the duck V's hopes to felicity.

But once for the climb down, must have been night-
 ly to go up,

          the lissome sang off. Then
   were enough great; to see another another
   with hammer, lark averted fares from well,
   pullings booned from her eyes

                  as too klismos
    from woozier.

            Zonked loyal ago, I
   spur full of then horns on and off. Far off
the stalks fell in cuss and gutless. Yes, cuss
   may be subtracted but oncoming hurry.

Still Be I Can't Wait White Flowers Backwards

Big drums. The air's not singing. Even me
Coming out of aught. I won't invite. Red flower
goop left her right cabbage green. From where
I am My attentions Straight with you. Have you
me? I thought whole taken for parts. Head home.
Right about now curtains. Down on you. Wade
In and kept hip if seen. You stand up On low
when you can. Of me Who isn't curled. Always
the look And then, Look, up Lasts for no more
a buzz. Will I leave With you. Over my shoulder
She heard &&&&&&& Cabbage leaves for me

fowl
like myself
& saw
Aught
Above.
Over us
in some
falling I
was small
& called down
to Aught.
She had after all
& the call,
she was not then yet.

I sit in front of
the strum.
I mostly occupy.

Still be I can't wait to be
sung back to possible.
Her with my mind looks into big drums.

Squished In The Sky White Thistle To My Eye Unidle

White sky islands Humming birds waiting finally

I say Melons Ons Ons Ons Ons Ons Sketch time White
circlings indent Clouds Hanging plants Language
to fill their shadows A simple shoulder
met everyone in the speak it brought I Letting me
know I am here Then away Uninteresting
thought White rose up the hallway Thick covering

waltzing lambs On her way forward nothering Brain
deformed leaf spent the winter numbering melons in
her plot sob alive blowing out the roses from her
out Growing end After end longer Human grass Is paper

for the eye leant to the sky destroyed the way Day I
watched the white roses wilt Death I do not know
how to stop I want my wander turned

You To The Light By My Chant Interpret

the gleam, window, existence. Alters made
out of breath maintain the way golden, so
usual finish won't take: bare being
sent with time unbringing. Small gem, be true
out, you to the light listening. Do it alone,
green step. Dead clouds have thought no color
to fill in. Their wander leaves the surface
alive. You see till the dead clouds change
her gaze. They are making figures, i-
dentical orchids, get up, drop. Whose light
won't golden the necklace under her hands,
her hands round a fixture. Body weighed down
by purple body, leave the surface alive.
Orchids, get up. Drop. Continue through pause.

Melon Puddle Take Care Of The Ducks

On earth

      dumpsters and lavender drool drifts,
a flower caves
        through my head. Why

      tell me now? No parachutes to this

or that chiseled cleavage up white below
the astro

      nauts' nosebleed. There's an answer:

Bedpost. Pestle. Hidden reindeer.

          Throw a farewell party
             then leave me to
languish in lawn.
       Let the anthill prepare

for better or feather and light. My head

pits in a place where
        hum takes off. Hear live

weather to make the harp leap. Hear the land-

scape filter fruit piles. Whipped up, there I

go to the distance. Weasel heads

      in mouth, bring back my body.

One Melon Ambrosia E A Note

Dawn: A plate of unfinished cake—an old house
with a modern addition. Flowers thrown
everywhere. A white layered cake in front
of white blinds. A golden plate. Love object.

Dusk: My dinner came with a full glass
of champagne. Naked except for a top.
Impatient Night, did you mean love? I read
the last word. I hurried to "Open." Blue
ink turned my thumbs into stamps. Day-old flowers
translated to the page. I forgot. Careless
Or want? An ending that is only
in mine. It has to do with my ego,
my ending is best and nothing else.

The world we love completely: storage.

Bits Of Sky Construction. White Begs To Be

With You. Nicks in the wall. Sugar packets.
Exaggerated Human Pear. Thud that
sing. The pause comes in thinking the Red
a flower-lush broth, green moon boiled egg
soup. Tell me you said once who wanted here
pouring from last spring. The last, this pen is
just enough moon. Bumping heads. Little x
Happy O. Involuntary brightness
goes to the tramp parked in the field I want
to know. Notice the rain littering the
lush turned into everywhere you and went
an ending. Unstopped. I do now life night
blossoming, invent never of its own.

For You

Look out for me
after night lugs away
the railing.

Beach Chemise.
Bills Over the Boat. Violet
carpet extends my face. My face
changed love on me.

      Shoulders. Or
      what went pulling it out. My face

jewels flipper for you. Look
out for me. You and there
you go, for you
bare leaves.

Squiggly waves with ladies.
      You and them neck
         deep, stems.

One Hand In The Fig Basket

Be hills.
  Be hark.
    Occasion in the sea slime
and mammal with the so on.

  Suck and arrow.
Learn the lingo.
    A forehead. A frustration. Lava flowers
here in the mad O.

I admit motion.

  Ponds bang about
the iridescent
eyeballs.
Call them lovers.
  When there are ponds,
    Call them hips.

        You unknowable.
        You tiny afterlife.

The lovers leave,

mulberry swim trunks, sweet
  sinking
  animals,
    wind chimes.

Each word sets off tulips.

These Normal And Tall, Those Magenta Fountains

won't provide but bash without
a sound, gathering back
by traipse
or close to a sequin. Everybody. We fail
porches. Our minds gist with puncture, our chatter
you look like me. The shapeheap choir
allowed to happen.
Weep when you, I sway
the sway even; everybody loved you, me
around the waist.
There is nothing in there. We enter tuft.
Notice what else breathes without
sometime bent in two:

Socket
Water unformed with magenta. Makes me
look, every
mermaid escapes you. Here, the egg
lace wrinkle goes to the snail to be half
way as stem.

Bright Organized Colors Go Off Next To

The Weep Stringing. Living wrong. A note to
describe the gift. It's me. Where's the on? I
remember the spider's web when I walk
through it. Up right. Away from my mouth. Thrown
belongings. A cloud wake: purple colored font i-
talics. This morning the way my head o-
pening to make never. Finger up, down,
up, down. Seams of color. Hand caught up in
one line souled winging. Breaks in the sky. With
my eyes in this morning's rain, my legs crop.
Sound with shape. By my side my day I think
one summer to come. Spring prepares a teal
shirt, a lime green sweater. See it→ sound-fill
doing day, messing my streak. Your turn you
offer me. Last time looking through the wind.

Nothing To Do. Endless Scatters By Sight

The Bulbs Already In The Ground Go On
By Day. A tune from memory: busy
signal behind your leave; I saw the sound.
Green tops the soon coming over time.
The grey pencil without an eraser I
kept from the hotel room. The snow yet on
the bough, nor sing. Open gate, you find me
a shadow to stand in. Could I be light's
prick? I'm out of it before I stop. Light
of day at every turn; unhurried in
this air. I buy a white tile for two
bucks: a sunblock, a cloud from bough to air.
A change to be complete. The unsure
earth pulls a sugar cube from its mouth.

The Molt You Dew My Head Mash Down

Down Showers.

Bright Sob occludes coal combed extensions. Out
again. The roof runs back more of us. I broom
the lisp around. Dark visit, sit. Is
she? The hair in your face comes on
full. With

the going curl, I'm the living gone.

My Quay, My Tail on the ground. Sap
Mass drops from
top Slender gusts. Honesty. Ho
nestly. Put a head on it.
I drink in. Invent.

Pearl

Broken Air Sing
      To Slow Heights Erasing
           Day For Pulling Out. Was the day out? Shades
down in the sunroom; I couldn't see.
     Anymore way? thought
my body. Queen Anns bobbing in

        white thinking formations—the peacock's relative—
        I see myself in.   Violet nylon drop. The
        chandeliers pop   one by one. My eyes
         turn back   at me.

Lay Me Down White Thistle

my eyes still beings drain.
The wind recites the background;
this only in of the world,
all come at it.

Viewless Move Further Up The Sky Bask Vamp. *

A tin can with a tropical plant—not *
a twist off. I crop off. Because no one else *
is here. The right exposure. White rarely *
appears white but usually looks greenish. *
I remove the quotes. I sit in a mowed *
lawn. I do not go to the lake, I want *
to go to the lake and jump in—rippling *
brain because floral pet. Loose light on the *
loose. I slide to the floor beneath the plant. *
I call at the dragonflies over my head, *
"You're not what I want to watch." A puddle *
remembers being snow. The one containing *
less white. Blot. See you. If you. From too *
many directions, white over emphasized. *
A few people hot on the same lawn. Unseen.

Dotted Blue Increase Trying To Avoid

the same way. Even in sleep out of path.
You're here; now going on. How do I
tell you love, No One, against the sky?
A list of colors forever. I be-
have the same way, even in sleep I want
to take to not knowing you out. Here,
what work of art is this? The next thought. See.
The strands of her hair there; there must be
light coming in. I wait for rain. Without
a fluent blue, a white stuck. You and the next
you. It's been a long time, how are you? Over
lapping everyday speech. The end greets me
and I think—long enough. What do I know?
Away from the wave a long breath from now.

Strange The End, It Cranks Dawn On The Breast, Rose

juice drink from our face, has a wonderful
towards, has a palace. Sun blinking to hea
ven. The Crotch Light To Step In. In Front Of
Us The Lake Struck Those Colors so to hear
Once increase On Your On Your spastic, with
out one another. Such OVE faith little
so more bulging into forever. At
the door leave us to keep early tinkers
in sleep proceeding a JOLT lace JOLT from
our eyes, sort the duds. There they are. That burst
distracts the leaf from its size, Offshoots claim
duckweed as sequins dripping answers;
OVE coding the one wild buoy. Our
selves still to come to wet Deep listening.

Wild Clot With Wind Out; Altogether Glancing

golden to surface, blurt in the sulk. The
length above elopes from its end. Oh whose.
Permitting slumber itself the landscape
the silence hasn't moved, off until I
could not see life let on. ACTUAL HY
PER BUT VIBRANT NONSTOP GOLDEN. Sow it
back! Rejoicing pleats pleat downfall. For us,
visible fails; left the wind out. Plasters
a downfall. Motionless. Next to the rain.
Sigh if not love low voices so last, The
World. Through the door The World. And here we go
into The World again. An unequal
length; linear linnets, intestines pul
ling my ears outpouring the circumstance.

Abbreviation Add To Their Height. Was

a palm tree in a sheep's field? Manage
the sky, the smoky garden apartment,
the table with the orange top, will it fit?

Confused outline—an arm around a grapefruit.
Coconuts. Bust. Why does it matter how
many trees there are? The opposite side
of a white flower. In the neighbor's yard.
Sectionals or trays. Oh, I need to go
shopping for ice without worry. A changed
thing on a windshield—plums without plum skin.
The was shaped as a balcony. Bust. Con
tainer. What every sentence includes the
setting doesn't love twice. All speech rehear
ses if. Coconuts compete for season.

Dwindle In The Hazel I Have Left
To The Bows And Bolts.

Lass the timbering
geodes that whiplash my hopes.

Climb under
my balcony, peel and sunder with me
the clamor of neon my eyes have pot-
pourried upon your decision to leave.

Poufs of linnet appear in our fret.
Amuck levades in the garths you speakfull
my balcony. Noonmumbles. Cymbals to
the weeds!

It's been so-so lovely romping
in the foliated ogee. Spending
an hour within elle, hocking pastels.

Bravura of pain, don't think the sane, scramble
up the blondes that try to bathe on your lawn.

Blurs For Both Beige Zag All Night The Sun The

Us coming unshapes of dust. Rush or to
blue. Fill out white square. I rest in the space
the day gives me nonstop. The leftover
shapes of circle wailing nothing to stay,
their chords at capacity. Grass tints plug
my ears. One cloud to shut it off, watching
us want tone. A handle the same hue of black
hardest to find. No normal human eye alike.
I assume I'm you. Ask me if I like strawberries.
I let the green decide to end. Lose its job.
Chew gum and smoke at the same time. Lie
down. Daffodils in a dog park—a need to
replace. The next sunset into remain. You
go, I'll remain seen dust in your low lobe.

Spot Sunrise: Coil Split From Skeleton

I have uncovered What Is Lowered And
What Is Continuing Out The Climb: her
under here. Our linger lacks branches—break
lightly; late being orange outlines our breath:
made love pass. Put up my noise. Doze, glinting
slobber balls, fessing swells. Beg the bark cease.
Heeds here too. I lush; alone I unwind.
Rut now, once figure which ends the entrance
hall. Why move to its tuneless anvil? I
cause eve; blue froth doom used for shade laughs like
it must, backwards by breath. Lank ear strawberry
curls hang in dew's width. Wait her form ever.

Hereafter IV Overbends The I-

cicles. Her The Finch caves in purple, pur-
ple fills foul. The breeze lets those balconied
strangle with the nocturne.

                              We turn our heads
from below, we watch moving graffiti
earth the round aglow.

                    Steal for hyacinth
Her The Finch, become your blood drops, a lit-
tle blister liftoff.

                    Face up in IV, hymn
hunt with we. No fig leaf, nor chirp, nor curse-
let be.

        I long my eyes from the white
ceiling so the body from legs. On the dead:
ice. Her The Finch goes out up from red.

White Drapes Between, Fill Up
The Climate. Remove

Us. Sanely
I struck
adhesive. I go set
out on a ledge. Just one
argument. Far out set by them
barely sugar. In the forest
now canopy. It thinks it is
movement. On a ledge. Pomp sets
well. Voice ahead of us. May
this thrill. Move at lilt.
Critters, weak opponents.
Geese make love to conceal
glimmers. Stop my head
all the same. A little ahead, white
between just one. So well
pines the rind of grass.
See instead of finger
marks. I live here.
Intervals. Kites.
Here is fur. All in black
before the heaven drape.
Hurl and soon a prompt lift.

Snow Flower Wag Holds The Day Here Beneath

a tree; to exist
the green is invisible. Arms dip in the sink,
      push the mud logged with furniture,
      lock and drawer. Water pleats
appear
by waterfall.
I'll rest too. Near you I can be
present, frond.
White kept at the surrounding,
stood looking, fit my face to see if I was
ironwork.
        Wader, your hinges
         shock the shape
          water's spilling; your legs now in eyes.
When I go mole, cover me.

Acknowledgments

Thank you to my entire family and my only David Busis. Thank you to Katy Chrisler, Montreux Rotholtz, Thea Brown, Simone Muench, and Lana Rakhman. Many thanks to Dora Malech, Cole Swensen, James Galvin, Dean Young, Tom Cable, and Robyn Schiff. And more thanks to Robert C.L. Crawford and Stu Watson.

"Nothing To Do. Endless Scatters By Sight" appeared in *Two Peach*.

"Till Morning My Head And Why," "Butterscotch Snot In Pine Tree Weeds," "The Honey Lump Watched From Here Goes On," "Bits Of Sky Construction. White Begs To Be," "Abbreviation Add To Their Height. Was," "Shake The Sing Lightly None Talk. Didn't," "Had Everything Without Shadows Unset," and "A Clara In My Throat Smash Wholes Us Lovely" appeared in *Prelude*.

"Loll Look Without Our Legs, How Artful" appeared in *SAND*.

"All Awning And Bugles, Still I Hope You Nearness" appeared in *The Iowa Review*.

"One Hand In The Fig Basket" appeared in the *Boston Review*.

"Voice: Red Turnip, Unnoticed Float, Crown On," "White Drapes Between, Fill Up," "Snow Flower Wag Holds The Day Here Beneath," "Wild Clot With Wind Out; Altogether Glancing," and "Whom Love Pries Paisley Apart" appeared in *Petri Press*.

"Ode To Gravity" appeared in the *Kettle Blue Review*.

"Still Be I Can't Wait White Flowers Backwards" and "Magenta In Bits, A Flower From The Ceiling Set" appeared in *Jet Fuel Review*.

"Umbel A Blizzard" and "Nautilus And Spade" appeared in *Likestarlings*.

The chapbook *Nearly Yes, Only You* (H_NGM_N, 2015) contains versions of several poems in this book.

Several poems in this book were inspired by Josef Albers's *Interaction of Color*, and the following phrases belong to him: "all normal eyes suddenly see green," "a repeated use of precisely the same color," and "White rarely appears white but usually looks greenish."

CATHERINE BLAUVELT is the author of the poetry chapbook *Nearly Yes, Only You* (H_NGM_N Press, 2015), and her work has appeared in the *Boston Review*, *The Iowa Review*, *Prelude*, and *SAND*, among other journals. In 2013, she won the "Discovery" / *Boston Review* Poetry Contest. She holds an MFA from the Iowa Writers' Workshop. This is her first book.